Magic

MINES

The Treasure of Love II

MANDEEP SINGH LOTTA

WORKBOOK PRESS LLC
187 E Warm Springs Rd,
Suite B285, Las Vegas, NV 89119, USA

Website: https://workbookpress.com/
Hotline: 1-888-818-4856
Email: admin@workbookpress.com

Ordering Information:
Quantity sales. Special discounts are available on quantity purchases by corporations, associations, and others.
For details, contact the publisher at the address above.

Library of Congress Control Number:

ISBN-13:   000-0-000000-00-0 (Paperback Version)
                000-0-000000-00-0 (Digital Version)

REV. DATE: 27/07/2022

Magic Mines

The Treasure of Love II

Mandeep Singh Lotta

1.

Dancing is my heart, dancing is my soul,

Without you I am a half, though appear to be a whole,

You now form the biggest, part of what I own,

That's why I always want to be with you, and never to be alone.

I talk to someone about it, and they call it a lie,

In turn they do tell me, "Well, it's worth a try",

Little do they know, that this is now reaching so far,

No one really understands how close together we are.

Soon it shall be heard, when the trumpets start to blow,

When the stars of the truth, suddenly start to glow,

Then there will be no speech, and everyone will be staring,

The end product will be success, of a recipe of, patience, promise and caring.

2.

All the time spent in your absence, is time that goes a waste,

It is full of thoughts and griefs, and does not have any taste,

Our staying away from each other, not in hours, not in minutes,
but in seconds do I count,

Think of how many times you break my heart, and you'll not be
able, to pay the amount.

I reckon what is happening here is the same on your side,

I tend to think the way yours are for me, my thoughts are your
pride,

I doubt you not at all, and to you it should be so,

If there are any in your mind, I am ready to help, but please just
let me know.

You tied a string to me, and left me to fly like a kite,

Left me alone to glide over the clouds, well, "Do you think this
was right?",

Don't you worry so much, because soon this will ignite,

Then in your praise I will keep writing, like never before did I
write.

3.

In this state of life, the heart beats in an unusual sound,

The outside may remain the same, but the inside has been crowned,

Many have tried to explain this, and many still take the pain,

The thought of decline is so strong, but will come around again and again.

He who has drunk from the pot, knows the state of it,

He who has finally possessed a piece of gold, knows the fate of it,

One who does not know his destination can never get there, even though he is at the gate of it.

One who's got this gift, is like one who has drowned,

To the ignorance of the people, he is actually the king around,

Riches have no value, and money is utterly useless,

The whole universe is yours, if only love you can possess.

4.

Up the hill, cold and tired, alone when I sat,

Longing for someone's company, but no sign of that,

It began getting darker slowly, moment after moment,

The streams of hope did not halt for me, but merely came and went.

I wondered within myself, whether day would break again,

Here was death that had come to me, for someone's sake again,

I did not at all want to save myself from this, because this would be my key,

Having the assurance in my mind, that it'll soon be you and me.

When we come together again, you'll know how much I cared,

How only to get nearer to you, even death I had dared,

I'd urge that we forget the past and think better for life ahead,

Rather than living in agony of being apart, we choose death instead.

5.

Longing for each other, were two hearts in despair,

Whose hearts were rivers of tears, and the hearts began to tear,

Then courage came to them, and they lost all their fear.

*They went to live in a far-off land, and this shows, to each other
how much they were dear.*

All people in the world give explanations of different kinds,

Showing a wide contrast between many different minds,

But whilst explaining it, some get off the track,

*As normal human beings I think, only understanding is their
lack.*

Conflict erupted and the two were left apart,

They were forced to talk to each other, just inside their heart,

Then the intervention of a supreme bound them together plain,

*To them were opened all the doors, they took their way and then,
no one ever came to disrupt their peace again.*

6.

"Why?" I ask "Why?" why did she ignore me,

Oh, I think she didn't have enough time to explore me,

I asked myself, and answered myself, and this went on for a
while,

Until one day, she came my way, with that ever-promising smile.

There was no need for talking, the smile just said enough,

I was overcome by this, and the after-shots were rough,

She stood there for some seconds, and then vanished away,

This was not the time to surrender, as this was the start of play.

When we met again, she looked at me with kindness,

As if a very big sin she had to confess,

She held my hand in her hand and said, "I'm sorry for what I've
done",

From today I promise we never part again, and forever remain as
one.

7.

I was gliding on top of the world, with the clouds in line with me,

We went over every house, field and tree,

I had pleasures all around me, but none answered my plea,

They were of no value to me, because, it was my love I wanted to see.

Even under the shield, I still could not be saved,

It was the storm of affection, that so badly had behaved,

Soothing was that tender touch, that left me in gloom.

I felt so weak in myself, thinking there'd soon be doom.

This was very serious and no remedy would help,

"Laughter the best medicine" some say, but no comedy would help,

The only need was for the one being awaited,

When trouble does arise, it's best dealt with by the one, by whom it was created.

8.

Trying to get to it, everyone's going astray,
Because only for small temptations, they're being carried away,
No one wants to wait, and wants to get there fast,
Unknown to them is the reality, of how the seas of love are vast.

The age of youth is when most distractions take place,
Everyone from everywhere, would not resist entering the race,
Taking silly decisions, a title they try to defend,
Following that windy path, that might never reach an end.

Some might seek others' help to get them across,
Only finding out the truth, when they end up in loss,
Yes, I say it's God's gift and yes I say it's true,
No need to rush for it, love will come to you.

9.

She was walking up the stairs, and I was following behind,
Having an innocent look on my face, but storms in my mind,
To get closer to her and talk, millions of times I'd tried,
Then, she saw my suffering and so she complied.

Have you no shame, following me at my heels,
I know in what you are, and I know how it feels,
But ideas against it, this cruel world has made,
The tree of poison has risen over us and we are in the shade.

Yesterday we were so far, and today we are so near,
What keeps us apart still, is this thin curtain of fear,
When one is sitting on it, it's not good to pull the mat,
I did try to ignore, but now I'm very sorry for that.
No one is now around, and promising is the weather,
Let's sit with love and put it all together.

10.

Our love for each other, I wouldn't have known bett er,

What a disbelief it was to me, when my dad read your lett er,

I was expecting tensions and argument, but all this went wither,

He said to me, "Bring her home one day, I would really like to see you with her".

Then I did as was told, and I invited her to tea,

Then I sat before my father, wondering how all this had come to be,

He talked to me like never before, and made me feel uneasy,

And the smiling and sparkling face of my guest made me feel dizzy.

In came my mother, who just said "Hello" and sat,

I wish you had told me, that the star you had said, was the star that looked like that,

She felt shy at hearing this, and got to her feet with a lot of contempt,

But inside she and I both knew, that this had been a worthwhile attempt.

11.

One in the middle of two, was one in the middle of grief,

One who had been robbed, but couldn't even name the thief,

The inside kept crying day and night, and the inside was a flood,

He said, "The one who finds my suspect, I'll shed on you all my blood".

He was suffering and dying alone, and yet no one came to know,

Still the sun continued to shine, and the stars continued to glow,

No one looked back at me, I kept calling behind,

The ways were so steep that the more I went up the more I kept falling behind.

Killing was the pain inside me, and I felt died out,

Only did I receive an answer, when I really cried out,

Now here was somebody that brought me back my breath,

And saved me from falling into the dark pits of death.

12.

*How peaceful it was, the bonfire, the swishing trees, the breeze,
you and me,*

The nearness of two lovebirds, which no wicked eye could see,

Whistling sweet tunes, was the nightingale in the tree,

Like the crows in the skies, we felt we were free.

Always on the lookout like a lion was my sage,

Getting ready to charge at anyone, who came to provoke my rage,

The deer, the rhino, and the elephant admired us with sense,

*The snake in the hole near where we sat, was forever ready for
defense.*

The robins made us feel like paradise had come,

The feet of the buffalo, hit the ground in drum,

Now the flow had become so much, that it was hard to digest,

*They understand our love and so I would say, animals are the
best.*

13.

If I demand too much of you, you are open to tell me so,

I'll then try to control them, and not let my emotions grow,

I do not want to hurt you, because I know your heart is tender,

Just give to me, that one thing you can surrender.

I want so much to be with you, but I don't understand, because
your words are deep,

But the little that is there inside me, I don't think I can keep,

My heart is tender, and I don't know whether I'll be able to tell
you clear,

Walking by your side is promising, sitting by you is even better,
and talking to you is just paradise, I think all this can tell you,
how to me you are dear.

For now I'll have to take it, but I am not worth all that much,

Those sweet words from you have really given my heart a touch,

Stay by me, I don't want you to move away,

In the presence of your highness I think, that's the much I can
say.

14.

That night when I rang you, and asked you for a date,

You had not even answered when I heard your mum say, "Okay
you can go, but don't be too late",

I jumped up in joy and put down the phone,

But most unlucky for me, my dad came up in debate,

If you're going out with someone, don't come in through the gate.

What made me wonder, I was a boy and you were a girl,

How could it be, that before me, your wheels had begun to whirl,

I fought so much with myself, on missing such a golden chance,

Then I reached a conclusion, it's my dad who always stops me,
then I asked him next morning, "Did your father like you, also
stop you from romance?".

The answer was a silence and he also came up in rage,

Like that angry beast, that had just departed its cage,

After a long struggle, I brought him to delight,

Smilingly he told me "Yes, my son, you were right".

15.

When the sun rises, I'm thinking about you, when the sun sets,
I'm still thinking about you, this myself I can't understand,

Your thought has made me dwell in the heavens, more than on
land,

I want to express my feelings for you, I end up using small
valueless speech,

It's like reaching for the stars, knowing well that they are out of
my reach.

Now, I can't wait for you, I keep looking at the clock,

I'm wishing for a quiet place, where we can sit and talk,

Mine are just simple words, but yours are fl owing streams,

Sitting close to you, is the fulfillment of my dreams.

Since the day we met, I've forgotten all my pride,

All I want now is, for you to be by my side,

I have reached my decision, now it's you to decide.

16.

With one touch from you, my heart began to rock,

Now I spend my time, just looking at the clock,

What has happened to me, I cannot announce like a cock,

I know very well that I live in a world, where love is out of stock.

Now wherever I go, guns and spears follow me,

I'm afraid of my own shadows and fears follow me,

It is no one, but I think a bunch of lunatic foreseers follow me,

Oh, what sin had I committed, that now, instead of courage and strengths, only tears follow me.

It has happened to me but I don't care a lot,

Because I don't see loss, only look at what I got,

For what I am told, bothered I am not, that day of splendour, when we sit down and talk, with you and only you, I will sort.

17.

I asked her for a date, promised to come, but didn't turn up,

She didn't value my heart at all and just let it burn up,

I felt pity for myself when I waited for her and she let me down,

It was of no use to her, but she had pride in her crown.

I had a friend, who very kindly asked me for suggestions,

From the face he looked like he could not take any more oppressions,

I feel so strong, but my powers I can't dictate,

She is so arrogant, that she won't let me see my fate.

As we went on another came in to join,

Those are just rumours, but listen to the truth of mine,

We were in school together, laughed and played with each other, but now has left me to mourn,

Hand in hand with a vampire, past the seven seas she's gone.

18.

Sometimes I find myself wondering, how this world is strange,

A world that is so self-centred and cannot accept change,

The people who suffer the most in this, are those that are inspired,

From time immemorial the world has won, and they have retired.

This still goes on, and still no hope is seen,

The world is still so primitive as it always has been,

Knowing this fact well, still their hearts out they try to say,

For them true is the saying that goes, "Where there is a will, there is a way".

The cowards will turn back while the brave will get across,

The ones who don't care what happens, and don't care about the loss,

Because they know one day they'll get to what they strive,

Because once a ball starts rolling, at its destination it's sure to arrive.

19.

Hope I didn't offend you, only to speak my heart I tried,

When asked what I wanted, only your love I cried,

But I think like a mere insult, you took it to heart,

It is not all my fault, your innocence gave it all a start.

Now what is to be done, we very thoughtfully have to decide,

Making considerations in a moderate manner, and not being overcome by pride,

If you think I'm bothering you, you are to tell me so,

Then this seed of love that you've planted in my heart, I'll hide away and not let it grow.

If you have thought otherwise, please let me know as well,

Because this is friendship and it is not good to rebel,

Let's talk this over, without causing any distortions,

Just keep calm, everything will be fine, and we just try to harness our emotions.

20.

One heart gave out, while the other received,

Then one heart was joyful, while the other was grieved,

Because if one had offered their life, one should have given some
care,

But sorrow sprouted in my heart, when nothing like that was
seen, my innocent heart was twisted and thrown here and there.

Well, looking at my face now, how do you think I felt?

Begging her for forgiveness, in front of her I knelt,

She sharply said to me, "Now I am no longer yours, and I don't
care what you say",

Throughout my life, I've seen many like you, whose lives were led
astray.

All I could do now was get up and go,

But made a little speech of attention, "In case you feel my need
again, you just let me know",

As I departed from her, I didn't look behind,

Then, I don't know why she suddenly changed her mind.

I don't know what to say, but what you said was true,

In my heart there's no one else but you.

21.

Speechlessly enough "I love you" said she,

I want you to be mine, and yours I want to be,

I want to take away your heart and nothing less,

That I think will drive me, out of years of distress.

I tried to talk to you, but time would not allow,

*Questions circling in my mind were "when" "where" and
"how",*

*The "when" has now been answered I suppose, and now remain
the two,*

Now to decide on those is actually up to you.

The world is in confusion, but question they cannot,

What I was almost losing, is what now I have got,

I was losing my way, but now have found my lead,

*I believe this myself and want you so, that you are the one and
only that I need.*

This I know too well, is a heart-to-heart connection,

*Where two bodies but one mind, are heading in the same
direction.*

22.

Standing thoughtfully at the foot but wanting so much to reach the peak,

That was our situation, when facing each other, we would not be able to speak,

Like a runner wanting to run, but having lost their track,

I was so confused, that whatever she said to me, I always told her back.

Like a gardener loses his pride whilst gazing at his flowers,

I sat beside her, having lost all my powers,

Like a traveler who doesn't know what is their next destination,

I could not reach a conclusion, having to strain my imagination.

Like when a bird needs to drink, but too narrow is the pot,

The more she talked to me, the thirstier I got,

Like a lost kite is trying to get to its master,

I was dying to get to my destination, and wondered, why it wouldn't come faster.

A very innocent look, I had upon my face,

Like one who had found all his desires, I finally felt in place.

23.

If it doesn't work out, just leave it,

If it comes your way itself, just receive it,

You love yourself the most, if your heart reacts, don't deceive it,

If there's anything you can give, don't hesitate, just give it.

Love in itself, would never ask for pay,

Also, with someone's life, it will not allow you to play,

If for love, there's nothing good you can say,

Then, don't waste your time here, just pack up and walk away.

The more you dwell on it, it becomes increasingly sweet,

What you have done once, you'll have the urge to repeat,

Keeping this in your heart, but wanting so much a treat,

Don't ask to be given, but give to love all that you can to proudly get to your seat.

Love is torturous sometimes, but is caring and kind,

It carries the brave above the clouds and leaves the cowards behind,

Let Only Valuable Emeralds always occupy your mind.

24.

When I came to your house, I was told you were gone,

When I went to the parks, it seemed like nothing was on,

Then, I turned back, hoping I'd find you there, I went to the
coffee shop,

You were not there either, even went to the club, my plans went
a flop.

I went to all the places that I could think about,

But each time I didn't see you, now this was causing me to
doubt,

I then guessed that all this was because of that unpleasant
sprout,

And truly he was the one who carried you away and took you
out.

It's not that I felt it, and I have to talk to you like this,

But all I want him to know, that everyone goes for their luck, and
he should go for his,

You tell me my shortcoming and I am ready to refrain,

If you don't want me, tell me, but don't do this to me again.

25.

Busy I was on the day, when all roads led to your residence,

I had phoned and told you so, but when I came to know, I couldn't believe the coincidence,

I knew the way to your house, and wondered what this was getting to,

This was rather exciting but upsetting too.

As I came out of the car, I heard you shout from the distance,
Was taken aback seeing your live appearance,
Looked at the house and looked at you, and asked you lived there,

This was like intentional to you, and little did you care.

I was uneasy and troubled as to what had happened to me,

It was your party and I didn't know, how could this be,

Having brought you nothing, I thought of giving you a red fragrant rose,

Your response was so charming it threw me to the ground, and for a long time, wouldn't let me get back to my toes.

26.

Gentle breeze, gentle taste,

Here we are, without any haste,

Because we know one day, we'll get to our goal,

Realizing this will show the cleanliness of our soul.

Lovers in this world, are like rats being chased,

This is no challenge to them, because they in the end are praised,

They are the people, who get to the peak first,

That is why, even if allowed, they never speak first.

Love is very brittle, and love is not a toy,

Love is utmost understanding, and love is not a lie,

Those who board this train, shall safely reach the station,

Love is not for crowd, but a two-soul participation.

If success is your search, give more than you take,

Seeking for the best, get ready, to die for someone's sake,

It is very true, that the ways are very steep,

Take care of yourself, it's hard to your feet to keep.

27.

All the bad eyes the world throws at me, myself I can defend,

Because I know, even if they'd like to, they couldn't follow my trend,

It shows clearly in the way they behave,

I can see them slowly moving closer to the grave.

You'd do what I do, if you had the inspiration,

Then, without me telling you the way, we'd have reached our destination,

Sadly, all you could do is challenge my art,

I knew this was happening, but never tried to revenge my part.

Art is part of my life, and it's what I've always respected,

You could not fight me, until into you love is injected,

So, whatever it is, say it to my face, I won't bow down for you,

Confronting me like this, would never get the crown for you.

28.

"Ssshh" you always said to me when I wanted to tell you this,

You're swearing to move away from me forever, gave me the taste of miss,

Then I said "Don't break my heart like this, just let it be in one piece",

Let's put our hands on our shoulders and give each other a kiss.

You'd tell me I don't have manners, and I don't think of what I say,

You'll be fine, but what happens, if they send me away,

God will have answered my prayers, and this will be totally fine,

Say that happens young lady, then you're surely coming to mine.

Then, after a little break, you'll manage to talk once more,

And tell me in open words, all those glories you had in store,

Your love was so deep, I didn't know at all,

I promise you now, your rise is my rise, your fall is my fall.

29.

Look at me in my eyes, and tell me what it reads,

Look me in the face and tell me, where my destiny leads,

Hear me talk to you, and tell me what you think,

Our being together like this means love is our link.

The first time you spoke to me, were like dreams to me,

The way those words ran from your mouth, were like streams to
me,

That your kind expression, brought warmth to my heart,

You know it too well, for winning hearts, you'd teach them the
art.

No matter what you tell me, I still want to keep close,

Not even as close as holding hands, but as close as my nose
rubbing your nose,

I want to keep day and night, tipping at your toes,

Don't be shy about it, that's how the train of love goes.

30.

Don't go away please, or all my dreams will shatter,

I'll do what you say, don't make it that big a matter,

I promise not to do again, what I did to you today,

Hey, don't just run away like that, listen to what I have to say.

I don't want to listen to you, you are very rude to me,

She embraces the world, and you are crude to me,

Take that it was a lie, when I told you so,

That you are the queen of my heart, and the only one I know.

You think you know too much, just tell me what you mean,

I mean what I've just said, and the outcome is clean,

Go get her here now, she won't have a clue, I can tell you that,

Look I'm only doing what you did to me, just a tit for tat.

www.ingramcontent.com/pod-product-compliance
Lightning Source LLC
Chambersburg PA
CBHW070957120626
46546CB00004B/1654

* 9 7 8 1 9 5 4 7 5 3 3 9 6 *